AN ARTIST ON
THE THAMES

PAINTINGS OF THE RIVER THAMES
BY

Graeme Lothian

EXCALIBUR FINE ARTS – CRANSTON FINE ARTS

First published in the UK in 2004
By
Cranston Fine Arts
Torwood House, Torwood Hill Rd,
Rhu, Helensburgh, Scotland.

BRITISH LIBRARY CATALOGUING-IN-PUBLICATION DATA
A catalogue of this book is available from the British Library.

ISBN 0-9547466-0-0

Printed in Singapore by C.S.Graphics Pte Ltd.

Cranston Fine Arts,
Torwood House,
Torwood Hill Road,
Rhu,
Helensburgh, Scotland,.
GL8 8LE.
Tel no. (44) 01436 820269

CONTENTS

House of Lords
London SW1A 0PW

I am delighted to be asked to contribute a foreword to Graeme Lothian's book of paintings. It is always a great joy to meet someone whose enthusiasm is infectious, and even more so when he has a talent to match that important quality.

Having fallen in love with the River Thames, Graeme Lothian has spent some two years painting the pictures which adorn this handsome book. To see the project through, he took a job as a postman and devoted almost all his spare time to painting. From Lechlade to Southend-on-Sea he has sought to recapture England's most historic river. Many of the scenes will be instantly familiar to some readers, but very few will know them all and so in this book there is something for everyone – whether your enthusiasm is for Oxford, for Marlow, for the Regatta at Henley, for Windsor, for the Boat Race or, like mine, for Barry's incomparably beautiful Palace of Westminster. He treads in the footsteps of some of the world's finest and most famous artists who, like him, were captured by the magic of the river.

I warmly commend his efforts and hope that this book will bring nostalgic pleasure to many and an encouragement to explore to many more.

Bernard Weatherill

The speaker of the House of Commons, Westminster 1983-1992

ARTIST'S INTRODUCTION

At only 215 miles in length, the River Thames seemingly does not compare to the giants of the world's great waterways such as, the Amazon, Mississippi, Nile and a score and more others. However, its location at a strategic time when Great Britain's Industrial Revolution was but a fledgling, then the world superpower, had a vast effect and influence, more than any other river in the world. This river has been at the heart of British history. Its strategic and cultural importance was recognised first by the Romans, through to the Tudors , Elizabethans and especially the Victorian age of global Empire building. The Normans, the last of Britain's conquerors, in 1066 built magnificent castles, which still stand today. To protect them from further European invasion, The Tudors and Stuarts continued the building of forts and dockyards for her defence. As recently as 1940 she was fortified to a huge extent to repel the expected German invasion. In fact the Luftwaffe used it as a navigational aid to find the docks and industrial heart of London.

Ships went out from the many docks to the farthest reaches of Empire, it being possible to walk across the decks of these ocean going cargo vessels waiting to being unloaded from one side of the Thames to the other. The wait for the unloading and loading would take days and queuing would stretch out as far as the English Channel. Today it is a different story; there may be still a multitude of craft , many working boats, but the vast majority of these are plying tourists and pleasure seekers. Victorians started this craze and the Edwardians cultivated it. Success of books like *Three Men in a Boat* by Jerome K. Jerome established an enthusiasm for leisurely weekends, which are still fashionable today.

Travelling the Thames is easy; most of it can be accessed by car. One can walk the entire length by the Thames Way footpath or experience it in perhaps the manner it should be done, by boat. As towns are built by waterways, trains are also an excellent way of pinpointing areas of interest.

It was against this backdrop that an idea germinated. I had spent the whole summer of 2002, Queen Elizabeth II' s Golden Jubilee, painting in London alongside the Thames, my large canvases attracting crowds. I was working away on the South Bank, painting the Oxo Tower and in the distance, the majestic St.Paul's Cathedral, when Anna-Maria Ash, one of the presenters at Carlton Television on the South Bank, suggested a series of pictures of the Thames in London. Thinking about it further I considered the Thames within the M25 Orbital Motorway. In the end the only solution was to attempt the entire length, all 215miles. It wasn't until I had painted nearly all of the London scenes that I realised I may have bitten off more than I could chew.

I thought the project might take about a year; it took six months more than that. The year 2003 coincided with a glorious heatwave over Europe and our summer, so disappointing for many years, came up trumps, enabling me to throw easels and paints into the car and journey off to the locations you will see in this book. It had a great effect in that I could complete a canvas without a long delay due to bad weather. For example the first painting, Tower Bridge, actually took me eight days to paint, going up to the location on those sunny days, but it was spread over three weeks, due to days of rain for long periods during that so called Summer of 2002.

Yet London occupies only a fraction of the sites I needed to depict. In many ways I enjoyed painting the scenes out of town more. Scenes such as Kingston and Richmond Bridges, Marlow, Runnymede, the world famous Henley Regatta, Windsor Castle, home of the Royal Family, Lechlade, the start of the navigable Thames, and the impressive seat of learning, Oxford, with its myriad of elegant dreaming spires. All these I painted, and learnt more about the subjects as I continued. Greats such as Canaletto, Turner, Monet, Tissot, all of whom have had a huge influence on me, have depicted the Thames in their own highly individual way, capturing it in the times they lived. In a very small way I am doing the same; in the time I was painting in London it was changing as I went from one completed canvas to another. The most famous of these high rise glass buildings was the aptly nicknamed 'Erotic Gherkin'- a story was completed every week. When I started they were on the footings; when I had finished so too was the Gherkin, owned by Swiss Re. I counted 24 high rise cranes around St. Paul's Cathedral alone, once the tallest building in Britain dominating all of London. Now it is in danger of being swamped behind modern architecture. I didn't use much artistic licence; if a glass monstrosity was there I had to include it. I did however reduce the amount of cranes visible, move the odd tree so I could see a church and made other minute adjustments that wouldn't alter the real view, but would enhance it slightly.

Now gone are the days of travelling in the guard's compartment of the train with a large canvas, easel, paints and all the paraphernalia needed for a day's painting. I got to know many of the guards and commuters who would take an interest in the progress of each picture, and now that it's all done, I really miss that aspect of the process.

I have included a text on each of the subjects to explain a little of each view, giving some historical information and how I came to paint it. The majority of paintings were started *en plein air* In some cases, when it was too far to travel daily from home to the location, a day or two at the scene capturing the tones, colour and light was just enough to complete the rest in the studio. Setting up an easel and painting in London doesn't attract too much attention at first; most people are far too busy going to and from work and the tourists have so much to see and do that they too are busy, with their heads in maps and guides. In the first two to three days, there isn't much to see on the canvas, but when the picture starts to depict recognisable features, crowds start to form. It is from this point on that concentrating becomes more difficult. A gathering of people tends to attract more people, similar to buses in England; you are left alone for quite some time then all of a sudden, a crowd. Then more of them and once more you are all eerily alone. At lunch times people tend to linger, casually observing or stopping for a chat. I enjoyed this aspect just as much as the painting process, and met an eclectic range of really fascinating people.

Because I live in Kent, travelling to the farthest reaches of the Thames for a lot of the pictures would prove to be perhaps beyond my endurance levels day after day, I decided to make colour notes on each picture. I set up my easel and working furiously all day, sometimes for two to three days, trying to capture the correct tones and light effect. Planning the best views from home proved a challenge. I bought quite a few books which pointed me in the general direction, marked down the most likely spots and set off. There was an enormous amount of initial reconnaissance, after which I was satisfied with the sights I needed to paint. I would then travel to London for the canvases. I always prepare my own canvases, cutting them to size and then stretching them. I go to my preferred shop, the excellent Russell and Chappell's, founded in 1776, situated in Drury Lane, London, heart of Theatre Land. Huge rollers have all types and qualities of canvas on them. I usually have a 'yard' of my favourite, Toby or Chris (artists' themselves) who work there cutting it to size, together with a collection of wooden stretchers that the canvas is then placed and stretched on.

I begin each painting using pretty much the same formula. I start with charcoal to give me the salient points, noting with marks where buildings are. The reason for charcoal is that it's easy to wipe off with a dry cloth; with pencil you can't hope to be successful first time and rubbing out leaves dark smudges everywhere. When happy that the charcoal lines, although roughly sketched in, are correct I transcribe over the lines with a hard pencil, 4H or 6H. Twenty years ago I would draw in everything, every window and chimney pot, this was because I didn't have the confidence with the brush. I was a better drawer than painter. Today, the roles are reversed, I am much more able with the brush and simply cannot wait to start with paint. This is the correct way, for me anyway, to start a new picture. Then try to cover the white, menacing, blank canvas with the largest of my brushes- you can't compare one tone from the other until you do this. A day or two later I can now start the process of putting in the medium detail, buildings, trees etc. Lastly, over the final course I put in all the fine detail with the smallest of your brushes, I use No.1 watercolour brushes. If I am happy then I sign it and preferably leave it for about six months to dry out before varnishing. In essence I don't really need masses of different tubes of colours, I use Burnt Umber, Bright Red, Burnt Sienna, Cadmium Yellow, Yellow Ochre, Cobalt Blue, Ultramarine Blue, Sap Green, Terre Verte Green and the most important of all, a special fast drying Titanium White. I could easily get rid of a few of these colours too, every year I add or leave out a colour or two, it makes it fun and keeps me experimenting at the same time. I never use black for instance, try mixing Burnt Sienna and Ultramarine Blue, or try Cobalt Blue and Burnt Umber, both make black but both a different type of black. As for greens, there are so many types of yellows and blues that the variations are almost endless.

I am frequently asked that painting in a large city like London must be almost impossible, not so, it may depend on the type of person you are. If you fall in to the category of shy introspective unable perhaps to concentrate amongst the noise and pollution, then you will find it very hard going indeed. I concentrate quite hard and don't notice anything or anyone, You tend mostly to be left alone if they can see you are working away avidly. On other occasions I seem to spend most of the day talking to an endless stream of people and not getting much in the way of work done. I am quite gregarious which helps, but if I want to have some time not being disturbed, I travel further up the Thames to somewhere like Swinford Bridge and you can find as much solitude as you want.

Finally, I surprisingly enjoyed compiling the texts, which accompany each painting. I found it was much harder than painting the pictures but I did however enjoy it. I learned a lot about my capital city and the River Thames in particular. Understanding a little more of the enormous history, the people and events that shaped our lives today.

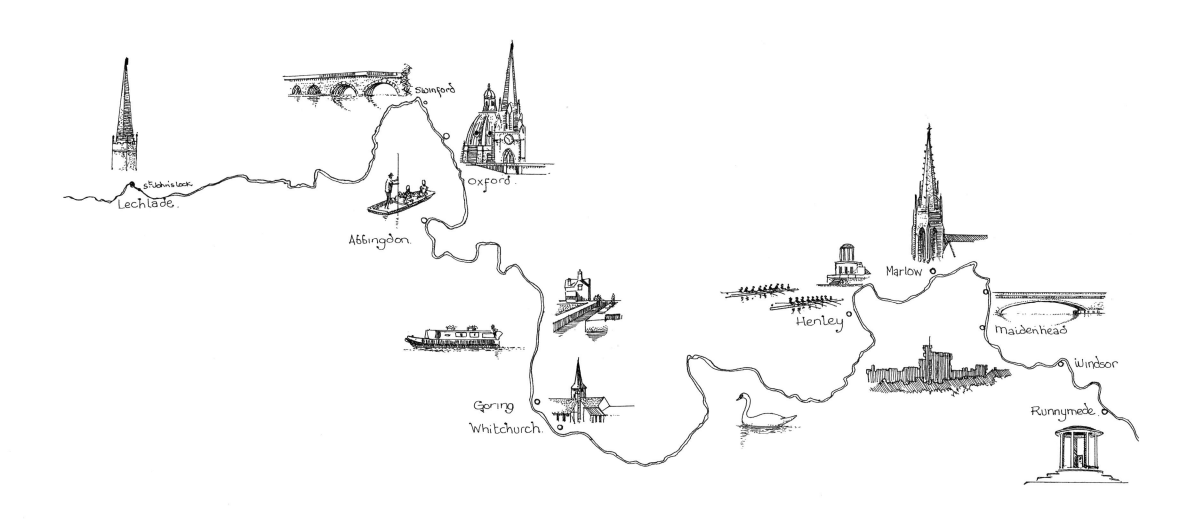

Lechlade.

St Johns lock

Swinford

Oxford.

Abbingdon.

Goring

Whitchurch.

Henley

Marlow

Maidenhead

Windsor

Runnymede.

12

THE PAINTINGS

LECHLADE

What a scene to start my artistic journey. The River Thames does continue on to Kemble some 25 miles distant, but Lechlade is the start of the navigable point. Lechlade (once Letchlade, which explains its pronunciation), is situated beside the Thames about 11 miles east of Cirencester, 12 miles north of Swindon and about 20 miles west of Oxford. It is a borough and market town from the early 13th century, and produce included cheese, coal and fish.

Inglesham, just over a mile upstream is recognized as the usual limit of the navigable Thames for motorized craft. Although it's certainly possible to travel as far as Cricklade, some ten miles distant.

St Lawrence Church spire can be seen for miles around and dominates the market square. Although the present building was completed in 1476, there is evidence of the existence of a church in the 13th century. The ancient Ha'penny Bridge was so called because half a penny was the price pedestrians had to pay to cross until this was ended in 1839.

The famous English poet, Percy Bysshe Shelley (1792-1822), composed his "A Summer Evening Churchyard" (1815) whilst walking through the churchyard after he had rowed from Windsor to Lechlade, together with his future wife Mary Godwin, the creator and author of *Frankenstein*.

I have seen quite a few photographs of different views of Lechlade but for me this is by far the best and an ideal place to set up my easel, away from the traffic and only the swans and two elderly bankside fishermen for company.

St JOHN'S LOCK

A little farther on from Lechlade, is St John's Lock; you can still see the spire of St Lawrence Church in the distance. The famous statue of Father Thames lies at the lock, relocated initially to the Thames Head at the source it had to be moved to the safety of St John's in 1973. This statue which sits proudly in front of the lock keeper's house was carved for the Great Exhibition of 1851. Characteristic of the small number of locks this side of Oxford, it was a marked site used as a navigation route at least since Roman times and is the highest lock on the river.

I was a little self conscious actually setting up on the lock itself, but spying a little secluded spot about 60 yards away I carried the paraphernalia there; it turned out to be ideal. Hiding myself in front of the bridge surrounded by trees I was left alone for the day, as this was all the time I had to capture the tones. I included the wooden Thames Path sign symbolically pointing the way east for me, and will be following this excellent path all the way to the northern shores of Kent, my home county, and the sea.

SWINFORD BRIDGE

The bridge at Swinford is one of the few remaining toll bridges in England. The present delightfully balustraded bridge was built in 1777, by the Earl of Abingdon, and even then, apparently, only because King George III, travelling at a time when the river was in flood, almost came to grief here. The fourth Earl was reluctant, pleading poverty. "Nonsense!" countered King George, "Charge tuppence a vehicle to cross and it will pay for itself!".

And twopence remained the price until 1994. Even then, the increase to five pence was granted only after lengthy debate and a special Act of Parliament, and *is* strictly to pay for necessary repairs over the next twelve years, although it's a nice round pound that gets you across these days. In 1785 there were about five stage coaches a week crossing the river here, and today there are something approaching three million cars. There is a small path that runs down the side of the bridge strewn with stinging nettles. I inched my way through to a delightful spot and set up my easel. What more could an artist wish for; the sun shone throughout, no one walked past and the only fleeting company were the passing long boats giving me a wave and pleasantries, all in all a perfect a day.

THE TROUT INN

A well known inn to generations of Oxford students, as well as hordes of boating holiday makers taking refreshments. It was also used extensively for many of the settings for the superb police drama, Inspector Morse, played by the late, great, John Thaw. Boats can be tied up beside the Godstow Bridge, you can have a beer and excellent lunch or dinner inside this ivy covered building, built in 1138 as a hospice for the nearby Godstow Nunnery.

There is no fishing allowed so consequently large shoals of very tame fish are near the surface, intermingled with numerous ducks. It is as rural a setting as anywhere on the Thames route. In the distance, tantalisingly, one can see the first glimpses of the *dreaming spires* of Oxford near here at Port Meadow. At Godstow Nunnery, the remains of a small Chapel stands. Here lies the Fair Rosamund of Clifford, the mistress of King Henry II.

This wonderful stretch of the Thames holds a further worldwide fame, because this is where the Reverend Charles Lutwidge Dodgson created the fantasy world of *Alice's Adventures in Wonderland*. The Reverend Dodgson is of course, Lewis Carroll, who was tutor of mathematics at Oxford. 'Alice' was one of three daughters of Dean Liddell of Christ Church College. He set out one July afternoon in 1862, along with another university friend, for a picnic. Originally called "Alice's Adventures Underground" this was the first telling of his story that afternoon. As they boarded their rowing boat at Folly Bridge in Oxford Dodgson began to tell his story, influenced by Shakespeare's *A Midsummer Night's Dream*.

FOLLY BRIDGE, HEAD OF THE RIVER

And so to Oxford itself, birthplace of the Oxford English Dictionary, the ultimate authority on the language. It has the background, as mentioned before, of *Alice in Wonderland, J.R.R.Tolkein , John Betjeman , Evelyn Waugh, T.E Lawrence, C.S.Lewis*, not to mention statesmen, pioneers, bishops , political leaders and twenty British Prime Ministers over the last two centuries. The pub itself holds a certain nostalgia as it was a favourite of mine in the early eighties. I included some friends of mine Sameena and Dina, both of St. Anne's, and Harry of Queen's college, looking down on the long boat, which can be seen trying to navigate this particularly difficult stretch of the Thames. On the jetty another pair of friends, the Reverend Doctor David Usher and his American wife Chasey, both of whom first met at another Oxford college, Harris Manchester.

The town was first founded in the 10th century and has been a University since the 13th century. The architecture and confines of splendidly handsome buildings give Oxford a uniqueness that can be rivaled by only a few places in Britain. All the colleges can be visited at various times of the year, and make for a fascinating insight into academia as well as being architecturally stimulating.

My advice would be to visit the three colleges who claim to be the oldest; Merton, Balliol and University, all founded around the second half of the 13th century. The inside of Christ Church Great Hall is now so familiar to many millions, as Hogwarts in the film *Harry Potter*. Walk up to St Giles then follow Woodstock Road; on the left is Green College, a graduate college for clinical medical students. A little farther along and across the road stands St Anne's College, founded in 1879 by the Association for the Education of Women in Oxford as the Society for Home Students. By the 1920s it was no longer confined to Oxford residents. The Society became St Anne's in 1952 and acquired full college status in 1959. In 1976 the statutes were changed to admit men, who now account for about half the students. This is a modern building, which is undergoing an extensive rebuilding programme, symbolic perhaps, in my view, of the changing needs of Oxford in the 21st century.

CHRISTCHURCH MEADOW

This view from the Thames is the closest one can get to the Oxford colleges. Christchurch Meadow lies beyond the banks of the river leading on to one of the most magnificent of colleges, Christchurch and its Cathedral . In the distance can be seen the church spire and the distinctive dome of Sir Christopher Wren's Sheldonian Theatre. Upstream on the far left stands Folly Bridge built in 1894. Downstream slightly can be found the University Boat Clubs. Eights Week at the end of May culminates in the traditional festival and commemoration balls.

I set up my easel for only a day's painting and paid more attention to the rowers glide past, watching the myriad of other pleasure boats plying up and down this tranquil setting. The only real bugbear I had, were the cyclists who flew past, missing the casual strollers and I by inches, and whose sole intention appeared to be the pursuit of speed.

A ladies' rowing eight from one of the colleges made life easier for me by obligingly going as far as Folly Bridge coming back and doing it again. On the far side, the numerous couples who hire punts and struggle to impress for the entire time of the hire period, always brings a smile to me. It's far harder than it looks and I was never any good at it. I was however, good at going around in circles and looking a fool. But I didn't need the art of punting to tell me that. If you look closely, one propels the punt from the rear at Oxford and from the front at Cambridge.

To the right of the painting and behind the tall trees stands the Iffley road stadium. Accompanied by a huge sweep of sports facilities for the use by the college students. This is where on the 6th May 1954 that Roger Bannister broke the four minute mile. Helped by Chris Brasher and Chris Chataway as pacemakers, Bannister sprinted the last lap on his own to cross the line in 3 minutes 59.4 seconds.

MAGDALEN BRIDGE, CHERWELL

Not strictly on the Thames, but a subsidiary of it, the River Cherwell flows north south. It passes east of Christchurch Meadow and connects to the Thames at the Oxford boathouses. As we follow it northwards it passes under Magdalen Bridge, with Magdalen College situated on our left. Founded in 1458 it attracted many benefactors and quickly became the richest of all Oxford colleges, which holds true to this day. The bell tower, completed in 1509, is of the perpendicular style, containing in its 144 feet in height ten melodious bells.

On 1st May of each year Magdalen Bridge becomes the focal point for Oxford's May Day celebrations. At dawn on May Day choristers traditionally sing from the tower of Magdalen College located at the Oxford end of the bridge, attracting both students and tourists to listen and enjoy the atmosphere. For some, these festivities can even include jumping from the parapets into the river Cherwell below. A few minutes walk along the High Street, opposite Queen's College and next to University College, on the site of the oldest coffee house in England, stands the Grand Café, an up- market, charming establishment founded in 1650.

There has been a bridge here since the 11th century, this one built by John Gwynn in 1782, was widened in 1882 and further restored in the last ten years. As with Folly Bridge, you can hire punts and rowing boats; northwards eventually gets to St. Catherine's College or to the south you will find St. Hilda's, which achieved college status along with other women's colleges in 1959.

ABINGDON

Another beautiful spot on the Thames, situated on the bend of the river that initially sweeps successively west, then south, east, and north for a few miles and finally southwards. This view, across the road from St. Helen's Church was an obvious one for me. The other view was from Abingdon Bridge, seen in the distance, looking back to the church in front of where I was standing. I decided that I much preferred the canopy of leaves from the trees, to give me a border for the painting.

The remains of a 7th century abbey stood here until its abolition in 1538. John Ruskin lived here for a year, staying at the Crown and Thistle Inn in Bridge Street, while he was the first Slade Professor of Art at Oxford in 1871. J.M.W. Turner painted two scenes of Abingdon, which are to be found in London's Tate Britain. Inside St. Helen's Church, painted on the ceiling, is a 600 year old medieval masterpiece depicting the subject of the Tree of Jesse. A little farther downstream lies the village of Sutton Courtenay. I mention this because in the small churchyard lie two famous Britons. The first is Herbert Henry Asquith (1852-1928), the last Liberal Prime Minister, serving as PM between 1908 and 1916. The other being a bit of a hero of mine, George Orwell, who's real name was Eric Blair, 1903-1950, author of such great novels as *Animal Farm*, *The road to Wigan Pier* and *1984*, written in 1948, he just changed the last two numbers around.

Once I had finished the painting, there was something missing, people. My friend Mark a postman plus Chrissie and Gillian, the two girls who do all my photocopying so helpfully.

GORING LOCK

A lovely setting viewed from the River Bridge. A solitary boat exits, watched by the ever present lock keeper whose white cottage can be seen behind. As ever, the gardens of the lock keepers are always immaculate, people tend to linger a while here because of the natural beauty of the setting and a small shop nearby, handy for ice creams. Goring Church stands on the west side of the Thames towards Streatley; it was built in the 11th century. It houses a bell, dating back to 1290, one of the oldest in England. During the reign of Henry II it became a convent and in the 1300s was remodelled. The Thames path alters sides at this point; after a time on the west bank it crosses the bridge and continues in a southerly direction on the east side. Oscar Wilde spent the summer of 1893 at Goring's Ferry Lane, writing *An Ideal Husband*. Ferry Cottage is where, in the final years of his life, Sir Arthur Harris (1892-1984) Commander in Chief of Bomber Command during Word War II lived.

WHITCHURCH

Whitchurch-on-Thames is a picturesque south Oxfordshire village with a population of about 721, lying within the Chilterns. Most of the village is designated as a Conservation Area. Whitchurch has an ancient and distinctive Norman church, St. Mary's, with its wooden spire. Across the River Thames, and reached by a 100 year old lattice girder Toll Bridge, are the shops and public transport amenities of Pangbourne. Kenneth Grahame retired here in 1920, after his son was killed by a train near Oxford's Port Meadow. Grahame began a story told to his son Alistair, then aged four, in 1904. Alistair had asked for a story about a giraffe, mole and rat. After a few retellings the giraffe became a toad and *Wind in the Willows* was born, invented on the stretch between Pangborne and Cookham. Other famous residents have included the society hostess Lady Cunard, founder of the shopping chain DH Evans and D.H. Lawrence who lived in a house called Kylemore.

HENLEY REGATTA FROM HENLEY BRIDGE

The first boat race in 1829 between Oxford and Cambridge took place between Hambletown Lock and Henley Bridge. It wasn't until 1837 when thousands of spectators lined the course, underlining the new enthusiasm for rowing. The town raised money for the Grand Challenge Cup, for rowing eights. The 1839 Regatta took place on a single afternoon but proved so popular with oarsmen that the racing lasted for two days from 1840. Since then the town has never looked back, gaining its Royal title in 1851. In 1886 the Regatta was extended to three days and to four in 1906. Since 1928 its increased popularity meant entries exceeded the permitted numbers in several events, and so qualifying races are now held in the week before the Regatta to reduce the number of entries to the permitted maximum. In 1986 the Regatta was extended to five days, with an increase in the maximum entry for certain events.

The view from the bridge doesn't actually take in the course; the finish is just around the corner to the right of the picture. But if you are to go, stay a while on the bridge and watch the mass of so many different craft cruising up and down. From Chinese Junks, rowing boats, motor launches of every description, from the bottom of the price range to the top. Skiffs, punts, canoes, right up to the huge gin palaces.

The races are held on the first week of July. The start is alongside Temple Island (also called Regatta Island) and it is an arrow straight course offering superb views for spectators, who line the banks on both sides all the way to finish line.

HENLEY REGATTA

I thought to get the real feel of the day, it might be better to hire a boat for an hour and try not to disgrace myself too much. I almost managed a dignified halt when it came to return the craft after an hour. But, "my cunning plan", as Baldrick, in the Blackadder television series would say, coincided with Mathew Pinsent winning again, so nobody, except the hirers noticed. Never mind, the photographs I took came out well, I would never have been able to get the feel of the Regatta quite the same from the river bank.

As we were careering from one side of the Thames to the other, two elderly gentlemen, both in immaculate shirt and ties, glided effortlessly past . They simply had to go in the picture and I'm glad I included them, somehow they are the picture and are the essence of the non racing part of the Regatta.

Without doubt the whole Henley Regatta is something to be seen. I was dubious initially as my preconceptions of boorish types with fog horn voices made me a reluctant traveller. But there is no doubt in my mind, that the British 'do' these types of things supremely well. Is there a finer tournament than the Military Tattoo at Edinburgh Castle, Wimbledon for tennis, the British Open for golf, the Grand National and the wonderful Royal Ascot for the horse racing, the Lord Mayor's Show, Burley and Hickstead , the Oxford and Cambridge Boat Race? The list seems to go on and on; Henley Royal Regatta is up there with them all, after all it is a professional international event. The last day, on the last race, a team which included Mathew Pinsent, the triple Olympic gold medal winner won again in the coxless fours.

MARLOW

An extremely pretty market town, famous, amongst other things, for Mary Wollstonecraft Shelley (1797-1851) who wrote *Frankenstein* here in 1817. The writer T.S.Eliot (1888-1965) also lived here. I had wanted to include the wonderful suspension bridge, designed by Tierny Clarke in 1832, but in the end I thought the view from the bridge looking down to the Holy Trinity Church, built in 1852, the bend in the river and weir beyond offered a slightly better picture. I just happened to go there when Marlow had their own particular regatta. Instead of the Olympic gold medallists and famous schools' crews, this one is diametrically opposite to that. The local pub teams complete with shorts, t-shirts, beer etc. Boats are made up of oil drums, bin liners and planks of wood. Amateur and fun, I loved it. I couldn't really justify yet another boat race, settling on this classic and fine view.

The only craft downstream were a couple in their canoe, keeping well out of the way of the festivities on the other side of the bridge. Seen to the right is the well known 'The Complete Angler Hotel', in a majestic position, it used to be called Anglers Rest, but changed its name after Izaak Walton's famous book, published in 1653. Marlow Place, which dates from 1721, formed part of the Royal Military College before it moved to Sandhurst in 1812. In the graveyard of the Holy Trinity Church, lies Edward John Gregory who painted the famous *Boulters Lock, Sunday Afternoon* 1895, a palette and brushes are carved on his tomb.

COOKHAM BRIDGE

This iron bridge, built in 1867, has great views from either end. Unfortunately I initially set up my easel at the end looking directly into the sun, suffering the inevitable headache with all that glare. I reluctantly packed up my art paraphernalia and trudged to the other end of the bridge which in fact was a pleasant surprise as the view was just as good. The Thames Path ends here temporarily, on the south side. One has to pass through Cookham Village to rejoin it at Clivedon Deep. The poppies add great colour and contrasts with the painted blue ironwork of the bridge.

The village of Cookham proudly boasts a great British artist, Stanley Spencer who was born in the High Street. His *Last Supper*, painted in 1920, hangs in the Holy Trinity Church, built by the Normans in 1140 on the original site of a Saxon building. It is also worth visiting the Stanley Spencer Gallery, the only gallery dedicated to an artist which is situated in the village of his birth.

41

MAIDENHEAD BRIDGE

I included this small painting of the former Great Western Railway's Maidenhead Bridge for two reasons. The first is that it is one of the most fantastic feats of engineering and construction in the world. It was built by none other than Isambard Kingdom Brunel in the 1830's . It is still the widest and the longest brick arch in the world, stretching a staggering 128 feet wide, with headroom of only 24 feet. The second reason is that J.M.W. Turner painted a famous scene here; he and John Constable, in my opinion, are the two greatest British painters. His superb *Rain, Steam, Speed*, capturing a GWR broad-gauge steam train thundering over the bridge, frightening a rabbit at the bottom of the picture. However, I couldn't clamber up the steep embankment as Turner had done, so missing out the same vantage points he had seen. There are now rolls of barbed wire, signs about trespassing and court action. As you walk away from the bridge it seems to disappear behind trees and foliage. I was beginning to get anxious about whether I could capture any type of picture. In the end I did a very small painting with lots of the local wildlife, which are in abundance here, and am pleased with result.

As the Thames path runs underneath the bridge, to the east of the river, the not too self conscious may shout loudly and hear the returning echoes, I'm afraid I did when I thought the coast was clear. I can't imagine what the residents make of it all.

WINDSOR CASTLE

The great and historic Windsor Castle can be seen for miles around in all directions. I think I must have walked most of them trying to get the best view. I was glad to go at this time of year, the winter scene allowing me to capture the profile on the horizon, through the bare trees of the castle skyline.

The building of Windsor Castle was started by William the Conqueror in the 11th Century, The oldest of the present buildings date to Henry II in 1165 and added to and improved by succeeding monarchs, most notably Queen Victoria, who spent one million pounds on renovations. Inside hang Rembrandts, Rubens, Van Dycks and Holbeins. Amazingly the devastating fire in 1992 destroyed only one painting. Now everything is restored and most of the 16 rooms are open to the public once more. It is also the largest inhabited castle in the world.

As for the town, the Guildhall was built by Sir Christopher Wren in 1713, with four pillars stopping a few inches short of the ceiling, a private joke of Wren's at the expense of a doubting Mayor. The Mayor had insisted the building needed the four pillars in order to remain erect. The spectacularly beautiful Great Windsor Park, set in 4800 acres between the Thames and Virginia Water, is a fantastic place to visit and picnic. I went back in the Autumn after the longest and hottest of summers, and the trees were covered in almost iridescent yellows and golds.

Across the Thames on the north side, stands the famous public school, Eton College, parts of which are open to the public. Founded by Henry VI in 1440, the college has provided eighteen former British Prime Ministers. Perhaps the most renowned was the Duke of Wellington, victor at Waterloo. Percy Shelley, Eric Blair (George Orwell), John le Carré, and Ian Fleming, creator of James Bond, were all educated here.

RUNNYMEDE

The name Runnymede may originate from the Anglo-Saxon 'runieg' (regular meeting) and 'mede' (mead or meadow). The pre-Norman form of government, the Witan Council, was held here during the reign of Alfred the Great, whose castle was in Old Windsor.

In the year 1215 King John was compelled to sign the Magna Carta (Latin for 'great charter'); unable to write, he sealed it. Known as the Great Charter of English Liberties, it formed a peace treaty with barons who were in revolt against the King due to his disastrous foreign policy and arbitrary government. This marked the beginning of modern English history, the symbolic establishment of freedom guaranteed by law. This charter limited the King's own dominance and made the barons more powerful, and all men equal before the law. In reality, this did not do much for the ordinary person. The Magna Carta memorial was built by the American Bar Association on land leased by the Magna Carta Trust. It was paid for by voluntary contributions of some 9,000 American lawyers. The memorial was designed by Sir Edward Maufe R.A. and unveiled on 18 July 1957 at a ceremony attended by American and English lawyers. Now, 800 years after Magna Carta it is in the able care of The National Trust. Set in an attractive location, there are two further memorials here. The Kennedy Memorial, given in perpetuity to the people of the United States of America, in memory of John F Kennedy, born 1917, and President from 1961-63.

The Commonwealth Air Forces Memorial sits on top of Coopers Hill behind Runnymede and bears the names of 20,456 airmen, who died during WWII and who have no known grave. This poignant yet beautiful memorial was also designed by Sir Edward Maufe R.A. and unveiled by HM Queen Elizabeth II on 17 October 1953. This was the first new building to be designated Grade I listed status after the war. It is administered by the Commonwealth War Graves Commission. From the top of the tower visitors can see Windsor Castle, Runnymede and breathtaking views of seven counties.

This is the only painting along the Thames that does not actually show any water, and yet this is a Thames scene; the river is out of sight from this view but only about 400 yards from the memorial, in front of the trees seen in the distance.

MOLESEY LOCK, HAMPTON COURT

I initially intended to paint Hampton Court on the Thames, but finding a suitable scene that I liked was almost impossible. After wandering along the banks of the river up to Molesey Lock I was presented with this almost perfect scene. I didn't alter a single thing in the picture; the only addition was Phil the postman, even the pigeons seemed to cooperate.

Seen in the distance is Hampton Court Bridge, built by Edwin Lutyens. Jerome K Jerome mentioned the lock in 1880 and the great American anglophile, Henry James, had a need to write about it . We are now 16 miles as the crow flies to the centre of London, but twice that distance along the meandering river.

Hampton Court Palace is one of the great places this country has to offer, not to be missed by Britons and tourists alike. For almost 200 years, Hampton Court Palace was at the centre of court life, politics and national history. Although often identified with Henry VIII, its history was influenced just as much by William III and Queen Mary II in the late 17th century. It was built by Cardinal Thomas Wolsey in 1514, with 280 rooms. King Henry VIII loved the place, jousting in the yard, real tennis on the tennis courts, hunting in the 1,800 acre park and of course, romancing and quarrelling with a succession of lovers and queens.
Shakespeare and Ben Johnson gave plays to Elizabeth I, and Oliver Cromwell (the Lord Protector) lived here. The only time England became a republic was during Oliver Cromwell's directorate. No visit here should miss the famous Maze, where literally you have to pay to get lost. You should also visit the gigantic Tudor kitchens, where over a thousand meals a day were prepared and the Great Hall where they were consumed.

KINGSTON BRIDGE

Historical Kingston, the coronation place of seven of England's Saxon Kings. Including Edward the Martyr (A.D. 975) and Ethelred the Unready (A.D. 979); the reputed stone of their coronation is displayed outside the Guildhall. Kingston upon Thames is the oldest of three Royal Boroughs in England, gaining its charter from King John in 1200. Perhaps Kingston is best seen along the river. For many hundreds of years the only bridges across the lower reaches of the Thames were London Bridge and Kingston Bridge. The 19th century stone bridge I painted here replaced a wooden structure which dates back to 1219. In 1745 this spot was the setting for one of the last recorded uses of the ducking stool; a lady innkeeper was ducked in front of 2,000 people.

The existing Kingston Bridge was designed by Edward Lapidge in 1825 and opened by The Duchess of Clarence in 1828. It was widened in 1914 and again in 2000 to accommodate increasing traffic and bus and cycle lanes. Engineers strengthened the existing bridge and built a new one alongside in mirror image, reopened by HRH The Duke of Kent on Friday 29 June 2001.

Houseboats now line the banks; bars and cafés predominate all along the east side, while the Thames Walk has continued from Hampton Court keeping to the west side, before reaching Kingston Bridge and crossing over. I set up my easel along the wooden walkway, to try and capture a few quick colour notes. The young couple having lunch and watching their son feeding the swans are so typical, a scene I witnessed scores of times throughout the length of the Thames.

.

RICHMOND BRIDGE

The first week in March was bitterly cold but almost cloudless all week. It was impossible to set up my canvas, even to try a small colour note sketch would have been difficult, so, armed with my camera, I set off for Richmond. Richmond, or 'Sheen' as it was then known, had two Royal palaces which were in use for five centuries, from Edward I (1272-1307) to Charles I (1625-1649) . It was Charles I who first enclosed and stocked the 2,000 acre Great Park.

Richmond Bridge, where this view is from looking north west, is London's oldest surviving bridge across the Thames. Before Richmond Bridge opened in 1777, a ferry owned by the Crown operated at this point on the river. Henry VIII and his daughters Mary I and Elizabeth I spent a good deal of time at Richmond Palace. Designed by the architects James Paine and Kenton Couse, the bridge was built in 1774 -77. The bridge had gates and at each end were lodges for the toll-collectors.Tolls were removed eventually and the gates were taken down, the lodges survived for another 50 years. Richmond Bridge has 13 arches. The five river arches are made of stone while three arches on the Surrey side and a causeway on the Middlesex side are made of brick. On the Surrey side the interior parts of the brick arches have been converted for private use. There were two boats, one for passengers and another, for horses, small carts and goods. Carriages were too heavy and had to travel upstream and cross at Kingston Bridge.

I decided that a large canvas was needed and was glad I did; it enabled me to put in large amounts of detail that I felt were needed to depict a moment in time when I was there. The men working on their boat, the cyclists, the lady with the pram who's looking at a menu, Chris, my postman, the Reverend Usher and his family, my mum, Sameena and myself carrying all my art equipment, easel canvas and paint box. I think this painting works quite well, your eye leads you into the scene, the Thames looks cold and still, a reflection of the sky above. The composition works too, part of the bridge seen on the bottom right acts as a border, the shadow cast from the bridge frames the painting and stops your gaze from falling off the bottom of the canvas. So too the lone boat and far eastern bank; they act as a border, yet I didn't have to alter anything, all perfectly natural.

RICHMOND HILL

This is one of the most famous scenes of the Thames outside central London. Richmond Hill has been painted by Wilson Steer and William Turner. Charles Dickens and Sir Walter Scott(1771-1832) enthused about it, commenting "it has an unrivalled landscape". The Star and Garter home on the hill, can be seen clearly from the river. The oldest surviving ferry on the tidal part of the Thames is situated below on 'horse reach bend'. In the distance is Twickenham home of Rugby Union. Around the corner, just out of sight, lies 'eel pie island' one of the largest islands on the Thames , home to Trevor Baylis, inventor of the clockwork radio. It had its heyday in the 1950s and 60s when it was a venue for Jazz and Rock groups. George Melly and the Rolling Stones worked here, as did Charles Dickens a century earlier.

FROM KEW BRIDGE

As I walked from Kew Gardens, quite unable to obtain a good enough view of the Thames that incorporated both the river and these magnificent gardens, the sun was setting behind me as I looked east along the river from Kew Bridge. The whole light effect was spectacular and a scene I originally had no intention of depicting became this painting, quite by chance. I tried to capture the last of the sunset's dying glow. I stayed until the last of the brightness had gone, mesmerized by the beauty and the extraordinary length of the shadows, creeping their way along to the far bank.

A new bridge, designed by James Paine, was built of Portland and Purbeck stone. King Edward VII Bridge replaced the earlier granite bridge in 1789 and was opened with a long procession led by George III.

In the distance can just be seen, the Kew Railway Bridge, opened in 1869 which served the London and South Western Railways. Just around the corner, unseen, is the Chiswick Bridge where the Oxford and Cambridge Boat Race finishes, right opposite the Ship Inn.

THE BOAT RACE

A surprisingly fun event, where it seems to me that the major part of the fun is in the expectation, rather than the 60 seconds or so that one actually sees this age old sporting fixture. The first race at Henley, was held in 1829, won by Oxford. Held every year since 1839 apart from the two world war years, this amazingly competitive event culminated, this year, by Oxford winning by the record narrow margin of only 12 inches, setting up a greatly anticipated anniversary event for when this will be the 150th 2004, race in the series. The idea for a rowing race between the universities came from two friends, Charles Merivale, a student at Cambridge, and his Harrow schoolfriend Charles Wordsworth (nephew of the poet William Wordsworth), who was at Oxford. The first Boat Race took place at Henley-on-Thames in Oxfordshire and contemporary newspapers report crowds of twenty thousand travelled to watch. The race was stopped soon after the start and, following the restart, Oxford were clear winners. The event was such a resounding success that the townspeople later decided to organise a regatta of their own which duly became Henley Royal Regatta. After the first year, the early Boat Races took place at Westminster in London, but by 1845, when Westminster had become too crowded, the Boat Race moved six miles up stream to the then country village of Putney.

Capturing the race on canvas is impossible, so, aided by my trusty camera I set up an hour before the start. All the motor launches get into position, the umpire lowers his flag and they're off. The speed at which both crews accelerate took me by surprise, shooting past in an instant then they're gone. The crowds were fantastic, one assumes they were from either Oxford or Cambridge, yet the only accents I seemed to detect were Australians.

To date, including the narrow win by Oxford in 2003, Cambridge have won 77 times to Oxford's 71, with one dead heat. In the last ten years St. Edmund's of Cambridge have had the most 'Blues' (22) to crew their boat and Keble College have had 18 for Oxford.

This year, 2004 I was especially privileged to paint the 150th Boat Race. Armed with tickets given to me by Steve Royle, the Oxford University Boat Crew Manager. I had positioned myself on prime spot at the excellent Westminster School Boat House, on the Putney Embankment, where the Oxford crew are stationed and prepare for the race. The weather was unfortunately exactly the same as 2003, extremely overcast, quite bad light with a slight hint of drizzle. For me, who loves painting light it was a bit of a challenge. As luck would have it Oxford lost the toss (as usual) and Cambridge chose the Middlesex side, which meant that Oxford had Surrey, closest to the boat houses and especially, me. I could then have the Oxford boat in the forefront and Cambridge on the far side. At the lowering of the umpires flag the cacophony of noise reaches a crescendo as the two teams run parallel with the crowd. As they were level with me, Oxford even after this short distance were already at least half a length up. About a mile into the 4 mile 374 yard race a collision occurred leaving the Cambridge boat with the advantage, which they kept, winning easily by six lengths.

BATTERSEA POWER STATION

The proposal to site a large power station on the south bank of the River Thames at Battersea in 1927 caused a storm of protest that raged for years. Questions were raised in Parliament about pollution, which might harm the paintings in the nearby Tate Gallery and the parks and the "noble buildings of London".
Now Battersea Power Station is one of the best loved landmarks after serving London with electricity for 50 years.

Sir Giles Gilbert Scott was commissioned to design the building. His other buildings include Liverpool Cathedral, Bankside Power Station, Waterloo Bridge and the classic red telephone box.
The building is in fact a steel girder frame and Sir Giles Scott designed the exterior brick cladding and the tower-like bases of the four chimneys, it is the largest brick building in Europe.
In effect Battersea is two power stations and the familiar silhouette of four chimneys did not appear until 1953.
In 1983 all production of electricity ceased, leaving the vexed question of the future of the building. To date some 20 years later and after many announcements of 'grand' schemes nothing at all has happened on the site.

This winter scene in February is from Chelsea Bridge, rebuilt as a suspension bridge in 1934, looking across to Victoria Railway Bridge. When it opened in 1859 it was the widest railway bridge in the world 132 feet wide and 900 feet long. To the north of the Thames and to the west of Chelsea Bridge is the area of Chelsea. Always a fashionable and trendy spot especially during the 'swinging sixties'. In and around Cheyne Walk there have lived a huge collection of interesting people; Sir Thomas More, Henry VIII's stateman and Lord Chancellor owned a palace here, in less grand quarters so too did Oscar Wilde, Thomas Carlisle, George Eliot, Dante Gabriel Rossetti, J.M.W.Turner, James McNeill Whistler, John Singer Sargent, Isambard Kingdom Brunel, Hilaire Belloc and Henry James.

WESTMINSTER SUNSET

The truly beautiful Houses of Parliament bathed in an almost impossible sunset. Painted from memory, as I walked across Lambeth Bridge turning left down the steps onto the Embankment, this scene pretty much presented itself. I left the buildings purposely hazy and ill defined just like the French 'Impressionist' Monet did a century earlier. Lambeth Pier is in the foreground and the wonderful Embankment lamps, which have carved fish at the base. The Embankment is a remarkable engineering feat, created by Joseph Bazalgette in 1868, reclaiming 37 acres of mud from the Thames' banks. The giant walls protect London from flooding. Bazalgette also created the District Underground System, a new sewerage complex and a riverside walk, finally being completed in 1870. A grateful nation knighted Bazalgette, his bust being incorporated in the bridge at Hungerford, Charing Cross.

LAMBETH PALACE

Lambeth Palace is the last survivor of the great London seats of the Bishops along the south bank of the Thames. This has been the London residence of the Archbishop of Canterbury since 1197. Originally the Palace was closer to the water and the archbishops came and went (where is now the River Police Pier) in the archiepiscopal barge. Lambeth, according to some, means *loamhithe or muddy landing place* and indeed the whole area of the south bank as far as Blackfriars was known as Lambeth Marsh. A small and perfectly formed medieval set of buildings, including a 14th century hall with a splendid roof and guard room built in 1633, which also houses the library. The palace has a rich collection of portraits, a rather fascinating set of variations on the theme of lawn sleeves, from Holbein's famous painting of Archbishop Warham to a splendid Van Dyck of Laud.

The palace has seen a great deal of violent history, attacked by Wat Tyler the proclaimed leader of the Peasants' Revolt in 1381, during Richard II's reign. It was attacked twice in 1640 by poverty stricken mobs, and Oliver Cromwell also used it during the civil war as a prison. When Charles II ascended to the throne it was returned to the church and repairs were then undertaken.

I painted this splendid view from the Victoria Tower Gardens, adjacent to the Houses of Parliament. For the artist the location is flawless, under a canopy of trees and in the shade, right in front of numerous park benches, so I could ease my aching legs. Standing all day when painting in London is exhausting and any chance for a rest is always welcome. I didn't include any of the ever present river traffic; all such crafts obliterated this magnificent church. In the Victoria Palace Gardens stands an impressive bronze statue called 'The Burghers of Calais', a replica of August Rodin's masterpiece. In 1340, the town's burghers surrendered themselves to Edward III, wearing halters around their necks, a symbol of their oppression. Their actions had the desired effect and saved the town and its people.

HOUSES OF PARLIAMENT

My first painting of these scenes on the Thames, taking ten days to paint. I set up in front of St. Thomas's Hospital, behind me sat or lay patients catching the warmth of the sun and watching the world go by. They would become my regular audience for the next two weeks, never failing to let me know if I was late; I could never be too early. At the end of the day I would go round to them showing the day's work, receiving comments from patients and staff alike. I sold the painting to a beautiful lady I had already put in the picture. Margaret used to walk past every day in a red dress and I was delighted that she stopped one day and asked if the picture was for sale.

The Houses of Parliament or 'place to speak', otherwise known as The Palace of Westminster, stands on the site where Edward the Confessor had the original palace built in the first half of the eleventh century. It was a royal palace until 1512. Burnt down in 1834 the building we now know today was rebuilt in 1847 by Charles Barry and Augustus Pugin. It houses 1100 rooms and over two miles of passages. The magnificent Gothic Revival masterpiece you see today was built between 1840 and 1888; this was the work of Charles Barry who designed the buildings to blend with nearby Westminster Abbey. The two imposing towers, well known landmarks in London, are St Stephen's Tower and Victoria Tower, on who's flag pole the Union Jack flies when parliament is sitting. Big Ben sits behind the clock face on St. Stephen's Tower, which arguably makes it London's most famous landmark. Entrance to Westminster Hall is permitted only as part of a guided tour, otherwise it can be viewed from St. Stephen's porch above. The hall measuring 240 feet by 60 feet has an impressive hammerbeam roof of oak and is one of the most imposing medieval halls in Europe. In this noble setting coronation banquets were held until 1821. It was used as England's highest court of law until the nineteenth century and it was here that Guy Fawkes was tried for attempting to blow up the House of Lords on 5 November 1605. The statue of Oliver Cromwell, which stands outside the hall, reminds us it was here in 1653 that he was sworn in as Lord Protector. The seating arrangement in the house is reminiscent of choir stalls, the members of the cabinet sit on the front benches while opposition senior members sit directly opposite. The distance between the benches marked out on the floor in red lines, is exactly two sword lengths and one foot apart. Members are not allowed to cross these lines, thus ensuring that debates are kept orderly. In the centre of the floor stands the Table of the House, on which the mace is placed at the start of each parliamentary sitting; this is the Speaker's sceptre. The speaker of the house presides over sittings, keeping order.

THE LONDON EYE, WESTMINSTER

A great view and only recently available to the public. A new footbridge was built last year on the west side of Charing Cross Railway Bridge. The other new construction is the popular London Eye, the huge revolving ferris wheel next to the old Greater London Council building. Built with sponsorship from British Airways it was 'the' hit during the Queen's Golden Jubilee, whilst the Dome at Greenwich was a disaster. The London Eye strictly speaking isn't a ferris wheel at all, the capsules are enclosed and on the outside, and the supporting 'A' frame is only on one side. It carries 15,000 people each day and with good visibility can see up to 25 miles in all directions. Built using 1700 tonnes of steel, equivalent to 250 double-decker buses, that makes the 135 metre wheel the highest in the world. To the right is the often overlooked RAF memorial to the fallen aircrew during the last two wars. Erected in 1923 to commemorate those who served in the Royal Air Force in WW1, designed by Sir Reginald Blomfield and Sir William Reid Dick. A golden eagle sits atop wearing the RAF motto 'Per Ardva ad Astra', 'through endeavour to the stars'.

This scene presented itself as I walked across the bridge to catch my train at Charing Cross, it was the last warm weekend in September and a slight chill was in the air, but the sunset and light was fantastic. The tourist boats had just come up from Greenwich to Westminster, the City Cruises boat now seen heading its way back to Greenwich on the last trip of the day.

To the right of Big Ben is the new Portcullis House, which gives more office space to the Members of Parliament. Next door is the famous 'Old Scotland Yard' the former headquarters of the Metropolitan Police. If you want a bird's eye view of all this, then go on one of the pods on the London Eye; you will get a fantastic panorama of most of the sights of the capital.

OXO TOWER

When the tide is out, especially on a Sunday, this scene is reminiscent of any coastal beach on a Bank Holiday weekend with cafeteria, shops and restaurants in front of the Oxo Tower. Hundreds picnic, sunbathe, kick a ball around or aimlessly wander along the sand and pebbles called the King's Reach. The Oxo Tower got around the problem of advertising on the front of buildings, by incorporating their logo within the building structure, all in a fabulous Art Deco style. Its architect, Albert W Moore, proposed to spell out the name in electric lights on a tower but was refused permission. He came back with OXO incorporated as windows in an elemental geometric form on all four sides of the tower. The OXO "sign" could no longer be classified as an advert. The windows shone out their message from what was at that time London's second highest commercial building. It was known as Stamford Wharf and was used for cold storage, processing and packing. Meat was delivered by barge, off-loaded by large cranes fixed to the building and passed through loading bays (which you can still see on the riverside).

Opposite stands the mighty St. Paul's Cathedral, built by Sir Christopher Wren in 1710, taking 35 years to build. It replaced the old St. Paul's, which burnt to the ground in the Great Fire of 1666. The 365 feet high dome is only slightly smaller than St. Peter's in Rome. If you want to climb to the very top you can, there are 530 steps from bottom to top.

This is a large canvas, and I set up my easel in the last week of August and the first week of September, right in front of Carlton Television Studios. This view sits behind the newsreaders. One of them, Anna-Maria Ash used to come down and watch me work, it was she who mentioned that I ought to paint the Thames in London. The idea germinated in my mind and eventually I settled on painting the entire navigable length. Little did I realise that perhaps I had bitten off more than I could chew, taking over one and a half years to finish the paintings, and a further six months to write the text and complete the drawings.

THE THAMES FROM ST. PAUL'S

If you climb the 530 steps to the top of St. Paul's dome this is the wonderful view you get, looking down onto King's Reach on the south side of the river. On the edge of the tree line is where I used to set up my easel, and painted the previous page's picture, two scenes looking at each other. To the left can be seen the Oxo Tower, to the right the Carlton Television building and the Royal Festival Halls. The two bridges are the Blackfriars road and rail bridges. The original road bridge was built in 1760 and the present one built in 1860. The elegant iron rail bridge of 1886 was designed for the London, Chatham and Dover Railways.

In the distance around the bend in the river can just be made out the London Eye, the Shell Tower and St. Stephen's Tower (housing Big Ben) .The modern 1945 Waterloo Bridge is the next one up followed by a bridge I know only too well, the Charing Cross Bridge also known as Hungerford Bridge, replacing the one before in 1864. Walkways either side of the railway give you great views up and down the Thames.

SHAKESPEARE'S GLOBE THEATRE

Walk across Southwark Bridge (1921) and view this scene from the arts, one visual and contemporary, the other, performing. The Tate Modern, an international collection of 20th century art housed in the former Bankside Power Station. It was built in 1935 by Sir Giles Gilbert Scott. Inside are perceptions of mainly non-representational , Surrealism, Pop and Minimal Art.The views immediately inside the foyer and the view from upstairs looking out to the Thames, are what lingers in my mind most.

Next door is the fabulous Globe Theatre. The original built in 1599 stood 200 yards away but nothing of that survives. In 1949 the American actor Sam Wanamaker found only a plaque to commemorate the place of Shakespeare's masterpieces. It took him nearly 40 years (work began in 1987) to reconstruct the new Globe. Built in a thatched 'O' to exact construction methods of 400 years ago. An open air auditorium where plays are performed from May to August, whatever the weather. There is a fascinating exhibition and tour that lasts about one and a half hours, bringing to life Elizabethan England. The first Bankside Globe performances included the new plays of, *Romeo and Juliet*, *King Lear*, *Macbeth* and *Othello*, with Shakespeare performing in the cast himself.

On the horizon, to the right stands the Telecom Tower, or in my day the GPO Tower, unique in its time for its revolving restaurant, certainly the finest views in London for a few years until the IRA exploded a bomb there in the 1970's. Since then it has been closed to the public, but at least I did go up to the viewing platform when it was open. Almost invisible in the foreground, is the Millenium Bridge, built and opened in 1999, closed after a few days because of the excessive swaying from side to side. It was re-opened a couple of years later, at a cost of 18.2 million pounds. It is in fact a great little bridge providing pedestrians access from The Tate to the northern bank and St. Paul's. Everyone unofficially calls it now, 'The Wibbly Wobbly Bridge'.

THE VIEW EAST FROM LONDON BRIDGE

Painted from the centre of London Bridge, the two weeks it took me to finish the painting coincided with the hottest fortnight of the year. The glare from the stainless steel rail nearly blinded me, but in the end I think it was worth it. The open top tourist buses used to stop right behind me, opening the doors the drivers would shout words of encouragement to me, all the while on the top deck the tourists would snap away merrily. Then the doors would shut and off they would go to the next attraction, around and around they would go all day long, I got to know the drivers quite well. A truly wonderful view, internationally famous, complete with a floating museum right in the middle of the Thames. HMS Belfast, built in Belfast it was the biggest cruiser ever built for the Royal Navy. Its guns saw many actions including the bombardment of the Normandy coastline on the 6th June 1944, D Day. Opened in 1971 one can explore all nine decks and 613 feet from stem to stern.

Seen to the left is the Tower of London, one of the worlds great buildings. The White Tower in the centre was built in 1078 by Bishop Gundulph for William the Conqueror. It covers 18 acres with walls up to 90 feet high and 15 feet thick. In its time it has served as a fortress, royal residence, state prison, Royal mint, public record house and an arsenal with a garrison. During the two world wars the tower again became a prison for spies and traitors. Amongst the very last inmates were Ron and Reggie Kray, the infamous London gangsters in the 1960s. Tower Green, a square plot, was the site of private executions of members of the royal family. Ann Boleyn, Catherine Howerd and Lady Jane Grey were all executed here. Her Majesty Queen Elizabeth II crown jewels are on display, with the Imperial State Crown incorporating a great ruby, given to the Black Prince by Pedro the Cruel in 1367, and worn in the helmet of Henry V at the Battle of Agincourt in 1415.

To the right stands Hay's Galleria, formerly one of London's most important docks. Today, it has been rebuilt and is a shopping and eating mecca.

TOWER BRIDGE

Tower Bridge is one of the most recognisable bridges in the world. This painting took me only 8 days to paint, yet spread double that to complete due to the terrible summer we had in 2002, but what a fantastic subject to paint; from almost any angle this structure looks magnificent. Designed by Sir Horace Jones in 1894, its two distinctive towers house the machinery that raises the *bascules*, (French for 'see-saw') each one weighing 1,000 tons. The whole operation takes only 90 seconds, allowing ships to pass through. The 140 feet high upper gantry walkway is open to visitors, offering a rare 'birds eye view' of this part of the Thames. The bridge opens approximately 900 times a year. Originally, London Bridge was the only crossing over the Thames. As London grew, so more bridges were added, but these were all to the west of London Bridge, since the area east of London Bridge had become a busy port. In the 19th century, the east end of London became so densely populated that public pressure mounted for a bridge to the east of London Bridge, as journeys for pedestrians and vehicles were being delayed literally by hours. Finally in 1876, the Corporation of London, who were responsible for that part of the Thames, decided that the problem could be put off no longer.

Two massive piers had to be sunk into the river bed to support the construction, over 11,000 tons of steel provided the framework for the towers and walkways. This was then clad in Cornish granite and Portland stone, both to protect the underlying steelwork and to give the bridge a more pleasing appearance. It took 8 years, 5 major contractors and the relentless labour of 432 construction workers to build Tower Bridge. Steam driven up to 1976, the *bascules* now operate using oil and electricity. In 1952 a London bus had to leap from one *bascule* to the other when the bridge began to rise with the bus still on it. In 1977 Tower Bridge was painted red, white and blue to celebrate the Queen's Silver Jubilee (before that, it was painted a chocolate brown colour).

Opposite on the north bank is the Tower of London. The infamous 'Traitors' Gate' can be seen close to the riverbank and once the unfortunate victim had gone through these gates, very few returned alive. A notable exception was Elizabeth I, in times of her greatest peril. She entered a few yards upstream from this point, but did manage to convince her captors of her innocence and thereby regain her freedom and become one of England's greatest ever Monarchs. Near Traitors' Gate is the Bloody Tower, where the boy King Edward and his younger brother were mysteriously murdered in 1483. Two hundred years later their bodies were found and reinterred in Westminster Abbey. On Royal and State occasions, gun salutes are fired on the water front by a battery of the Honourable Artillery Company.

LONDON MARATHON

To get the best view of the worlds largest marathon, walk across Tower Bridge, part of the 26 miles also includes the bridge, and look down below to the Tower of London. Within months in 1979, hours after having run the New York Marathon, the former Olympic champion Chris Brasher wrote an article for The Observer newspaper which began: "To believe this story you must believe that the human race be one joyous family, working together, laughing together, achieving the impossible". Enchanted with the sight of people coming together for such an occasion, he concluded questioning "whether London could stage such a festival?" The London Marathon was born, with Brasher making trips to America to study the race organisation and finance of big city marathons such as New York and Boston, the oldest in the world. He secured a contract with Gillette of £50,000, established the organisation's charitable status, and set down six main aims for the event, which he not only hoped would echo the scenes he had witnessed in New York, but also put Britain firmly on the map as a country capable of organising major events.

His vision was realised on 29 March 1981, with the inaugural London Marathon proving an instant success. More than 20,000 people applied to run, 7,747 were accepted and 6,255 crossed the finish line on Constitution Hill as cheering crowds lined the route. Now at capacity, a total of 46,500 were accepted from a record 80,500 applicants, with 32,563 finishing on the day. To date more than half a million people have completed the Marathon.

In its history, the course has remained relatively constant with the finish being the main point of change. Moving from Constitution Hill to Westminster Bridge in 1982, it stayed there until restoration work in 1993 saw it relocated to The Mall where it has remained to date. These changes have necessitated route shifts to accommodate the full 26.2 mile distance while the building work around Canary Wharf also brought about slight variations. The start however has always been on Blackheath Common and Greenwich Park, with the route as a whole designed to follow the Thames as closely as possible and finish in the heart of the capital.

PROSPECT OF WHITBY

Built in 1520, during the reign of Henry VIII, this well known pub got its name from the coal carrying vessels from Whitby. Charles Dickens used to frequent the pub, Whistler and J.M.W.Turner painted scenes from the veranda. Originally the locals used to call it the 'Devil's Inn' because of the shady clientele and villains who used to drink here. A restaurant was opened in the 1950s and celebrities such as Princess Margaret and Crown Prince Ranier of Monaco used to visit.

Whistler, the famous American artist, whose wonderful sketches show what it was like at that time. Today the warehouses are gone, converted into flats, even the pubs are 'themed'. Gone too are the lightermen and dockers, in are the tourists and the local flat dwellers. Purely from the artist's eye, this regenerated stretch of the Thames with the no doubt, award winning penthouses lining the banks, does seem to be a bit characterless. One can only imagine what the view was like a hundred years ago when tall ships masts lined the Thames horizon, all the way out to the county coasts of Essex, Kent and the sea. It must have been a glorious sight.

CAPTAIN KIDD

This 17th Century building, which has been a pub for a hundred years was used by tradesmen making boats, repairing sails and working on the river. The pub took its name from a colourful character, Captain William Kidd. He was a Scottish colonial ship owner in the 1690s in New York. He became a 'privateer', someone who hunts and captures pirates, and then became a pirate himself. Eventually arrested, convicted and hanged at Wapping on 23 May 1701. The first attempt to hang him failed, the rope snapped, the second was more successful. His body lay there for three tides to wash over him, then it was 'tarred' (for preservation) and placed in a 'gibbet' for public display at Tilbury Point, to discourage other pirates.

CANARY WHARF

A scene unrecognizable only a few years ago, and I'm sure will look vastly different in a few years to come. The tallest building is the 850ft Canada Wharf Tower, the highest in Europe. Designed by the architect Cesar Pelli, the whole Canary Wharf occupies an area, once in a state of disrepair and neglect, of 71 acres. Now with enormous regeneration, companies have moved their offices here, becoming one of the world's most prestigious addresses. A little bit of America, in London. This view is from the middle of the Thames between Shadwell Basin and Limehouse Reach, catch a boat either from Westminster to Greenwhich or vice-versa. Apart from the spectacle of seeing London passing by in front of you, the other great reason is to listen to the fantastic commentary from the boats' captains, you'll find more information here than in most guide books, and infinitely more amusing. There are so many buildings and views I simply couldn't put, look for the Monument, a tall column erected to pinpoint where the Great Fire of 1666 had started, or St. Bride's Church which looks remarkably like a wedding cake. The *Cutty Sark*, the fastest tea clipper ship in the 1800s. All these and so much more can be seen from these hour long boat rides.

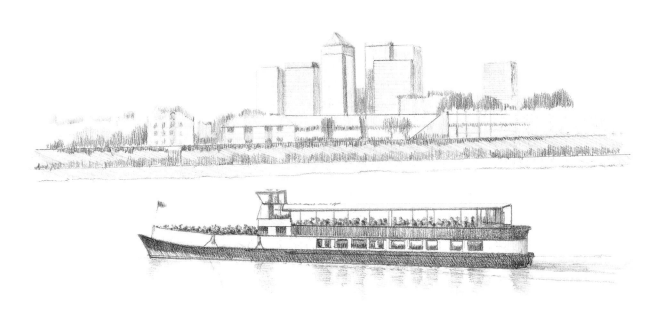

GREENWICH, ISLE OF DOGS

Standing on top of Greenwich Hill is the Greenwich Observatory, founded in 1675 during Charles II's reign. It was designed by Sir Christopher Wren, a keen astronomer himself. The observatory is positioned at Longitude 0° and is recognized throughout the world in the horological expression GMT (Greenwich Mean Time). At the foot of the hill is the Royal Naval College, also begun during the reign of Charles II. It was a Royal Palace for many years until 1873 when the college moved here from Portsmouth. In 1998 the Royal Navy moved from here and handed it over to the Greenwich Foundation. This outstanding view is one of the best in London. Situated at Greenwich is the *Cutty Sark*, one of the great tea and wool sailing clippers. Her fastest recorded time was from China in 1871, taking only 107 days. Close by stands the 54 foot *Gipsy Moth IV*, the yacht in which Sir Francis Chichester made his solo circumnavigation of the world in 1966.

On the far side of the Thames is the very much changed Isle of Dogs It is actually a peninsular but altered to an island in 1800-1802 when the Great West India Dock was built slicing across the top. There are various stories as to its name, some say it is because Henry VIII kept his kennels there, others that it was the 'Isle of Ducks' and the name has been corrupted. Go to see the London Visitor Centre which tells you all about the history of the docks up to the present day. To the left in the distance can be seen the Nat. West Tower and the building of the 'erotic gherkin', only half completed when I painted this scene. On the right stands forlornly the Millenium Dome, comprising a translucent canopy made from 328,100 square feet of fabric. It is held up by 43 miles of high strength cables, suspended from 12 vast 105 tonne yellow steel masks. It cost millions of pounds and was supposed to be a celebration of Britain in the millenium, but closed within a year because of poor visitor numbers. It did, however, have an ambitious but failed attempted diamond robbery, adding some rare excitement to this project.

LONDON FROM THE AIR

I had the choice when I flew to Europe, of flying from London City Airport or Heathrow, no contest. The City Airport is a super little airport right in the centre of London. The majority of the clientele are business people, I was just about the only one not in a suit, and definitely the only one with a camera slung around my neck. Luck proved to be mine as I sat on the best side of the plane, looking down on all the sights I had painted or was about to paint. We were airborne over the Thames Flood Barrier, Tower Bridge, Tower of London and the top of the impressive Canary Wharf complex. I was the only one snapping away with a camera, everyone else, I'm sure, feigns boredom at this critical time, when the aircraft is gaining height, but I bet I'm not the only one who's at least a little worried.

If you are one of those who's been up in an aircraft or balloon, it's always a sense of wonder how things look so very different up there. The Thames is a meandering, wriggling, brown waterway with the odd splash of white as boats chug up and down its length.

For a painter who's known more for his aviation art, I'm always fascinated by the clouds and the way their shadows are thrown on to the landscape below. Seen from above, there are whole areas cast in shadows and some in brilliant sunshine, glass catching the suns rays and in the distance where the environs of London peter out, the green and brown patchwork quilt of the English countryside begins. Looking around me in the plane I noticed that not one person was bothering to take in this awe inspiring sight, perhaps they had seen it so many times, whereas I admittedly was taking in my first view.

THAMES FLOOD BARRIER

Due to changes in the course of the river and London sinking at a predictable rate, a barrier was built at Greenwich to stop the river rising and flooding the Thames Estuary and London itself. Over the last 150 years numerous floods have taken place, the worst being in 1928 when 14 drowned and 4,000 were made homeless. The gates of the barrier lie flat on the river bed and can be raised in 30 minutes to form a dam across the Thames. In 1972 the government decided to build a flood barrier to protect London from the floods caused by storms and high tides. The last flood in 1956 had been devastating. The barrier was completed in 1986 at a cost of 370 million pounds; each gate weighs 3000 tonnes and is equivalent to a five story building in height.

Sightseers can take a boat trip down to the flood barrier. When I went, the vessel I was on was called the *Dunkirk* named because this was one of the 'little boats' that rescued the majority of the BEF (British Expeditionary Force) from the beaches of Dunkirk in the spring of 1940. Apart from the Royal Navy, hundreds of small privately owned craft set sail across the Channel picking up their 'pongos' (soldiers), thus saving a large proportion of the British Army from the, at that time, all conquering German Army. This is a beautiful boat owned and run by a family concern. Built originally for the Oxford and Cambridge boat race, it was designed especially to keep the 'wash' behind the boat to a minimum.

THAMES ESTUARY FROM THE AIR

Past the Thames Flood Barrier the river gets a lot less scenically interesting, there are a growing number of large industrial complexes that litter the banks on both sides, all the way through to and past the Queen Elizabeth II Bridge at Dartford. After we had left the City Airport we banked sharply and headed due east down the Thames, not quite believing my luck I snapped away merrily. The home counties of Essex, to the north of the Thames and my home county of Kent, to the south are the last pieces of land that the Thames negotiates before entering the sea. The river, naturally at its widest at this point dwarfs a ship heading out to the English Channel. On both sides there are huge tracts of low lying marshland, protected by great sea walls which are being raised continuously since the 13th century, as London and the surrounding land sinks at the rate of 13 inches every century.

95

FROM TILBURY TOWARDS GRAVESEND

From Tilbury Fort, which stands on the north shore of the emerging Thames estuary, one looks due south and can see the town of Gravesend on the far bank, in the county of Kent. The day I went to paint was blustery and with squally showers of rain. Most people think that it's impossible to paint in the rain, all the colours are going to run, they forget that it's not watercolours but oil based paints, which never run. I have painted in practically all weathers, including driving sleet and snow. Standing on the ramparts of Tilbury Fort trying to keep my easel from blowing away was the hardest part, but at least I just about managed to get a good representation of a bleak and wintry day in an industrial part the River Thames.

Tilbury Fort had its origins in Henry VIII's time, when a small structure was erected here in 1539. The present fort dates to the 1670s, constructed for Charles II at a time of threatened attacks by the French and Dutch. In fact the Dutch did land here in 1667, destroying part of Tilbury church. Tilbury is famous for the gathering of some 2000 Englishmen on the 8th and 9th August 1588 to fight the Spanish, in case Sir Francis Drake had been unable to defeat the Armada. Elizabeth I, gave one of those rousing, uplifting speeches that have been immortalized in history forever, the first great speech recorded by a monarch "I know I have a body of a weak and feeble woman, but I have the heart and stomach of a King and a King of England too – and think full scorn that Spain or any prince of Europe should dare invade the borders of my realm, to which rather dishonour, I myself will take up arms". " I know it was 'spin'," says the historian Simon Schama, " but it was 'spin' for England." It worked, Drake won and the weather, as always, was on our side.

Gravesend on the opposite shore was an old port and fishing town, the relentless development of the 20th century has altered dramatically all the London overspill towns along this coastal region. It was here in 1617 that Pocohontas died, on the eve of her departure to America. She is buried in the riverside Saint George's Church and a statue was erected a few years ago in the town centre.

SOUTHEND ON SEA

A rather small fashionable town pre 1840s, but after the railway arrived 10 years later a rapid growth and with expansion the modern Southend spread out along the coast subsuming other hamlets and villages. A mass of fish and chip shops predominate and it can boast the longest pleasure pier in the world. First built in 1889 the iron pier has had many extensions added to it, mainly to accommodate the increasing number of steamboats that were visiting. The final extension in 1927 was called the Prince George Extension, culminating in the grand length of 1.34 miles (2km), 2360 yards. There is a 'Golden Mile' of amusement arcades and the Kursaal building houses a bowling alley, dance hall, arcades and bars. The May Airshow is excellent and free, as the performing planes do their aerobatics out along the coast, directly in front of the crowd.

This part of the County of Essex is the culmination for me of many months of painting the length of this great and historic river. The painting coincidentally and fittingly is the last I worked on, started the last week of February and finished the first week of March. I realise that I have missed a lot of other excellent subjects that I could easily have painted, but you have to draw the line somewhere and forty three paintings for an initial attempt is enough for me. It is a most suitable number in this instance too as I was forty three years old when I was finishing the Southend on Sea painting.

99

ACKNOWLEDGEMENTS

There are as always people to thank. The first and foremost must be to Dr. Sameena Shakoor, it was her computer and endless patience in showing me how to use it, to which I am indebted. You will also spot her in quite a few of the paintings, complaining that I have given her size 14 feet in the *Molesey Lock* picture, I think she may be right. My gratitude must go to Sameena and Trever Adams who proof read the initial error strewn texts so magnificently. I must thank Sandra and Stuart, from the Sevenoaks Art Shop,who have helped me over the years, my very own SAS. My mum, Pat for her continuing support. Also, thanks must go to Dennis at the Framing Centre in Tunbridge Wells, whose team frame and show my prints in their window so expertly. So too the Francis Isles Gallery in Rochester, exhibitors of my originals who continue to support me. They have a unique non stuffy, friendly and superb gallery in the High Street run by Nettie, her sisters and her Mum.

My sincere thanks must go to David Higgins of the excellent Cranston Fine Arts, predominately a military art company, one of the largest in the world. He is one of my best benefactors, patrons and co publisher of this book.

I am extremely grateful to the super efficient Pamela Ang of C S Graphics in Singapore, printers of this book.

Great thanks must also go to Lord Weatherill, he kindly provided the foreword, to which I am indebted, but also the wonderful help he has given to me in the final preparations of this book. His legendary charm and humour in meeting him for the first time put me at ease in his spectacular home in Kent.